An Exploration in

Color Field

By Megan Delzell

I attempt to deconstruct an image into textures, colors, and forms. By breaking down a recognized form, the image focuses on simplicity and fundamentals. By examining the relationships between parts of the whole, each image can be an individual work, and a piece of a work.

Using historical forms of photography, such as Polaroids and infrared film, works can come together and merge in an appreciation of imperfection and texture. Past and present can embrace to create a process that is unique with each composition.

-Megan Delzell

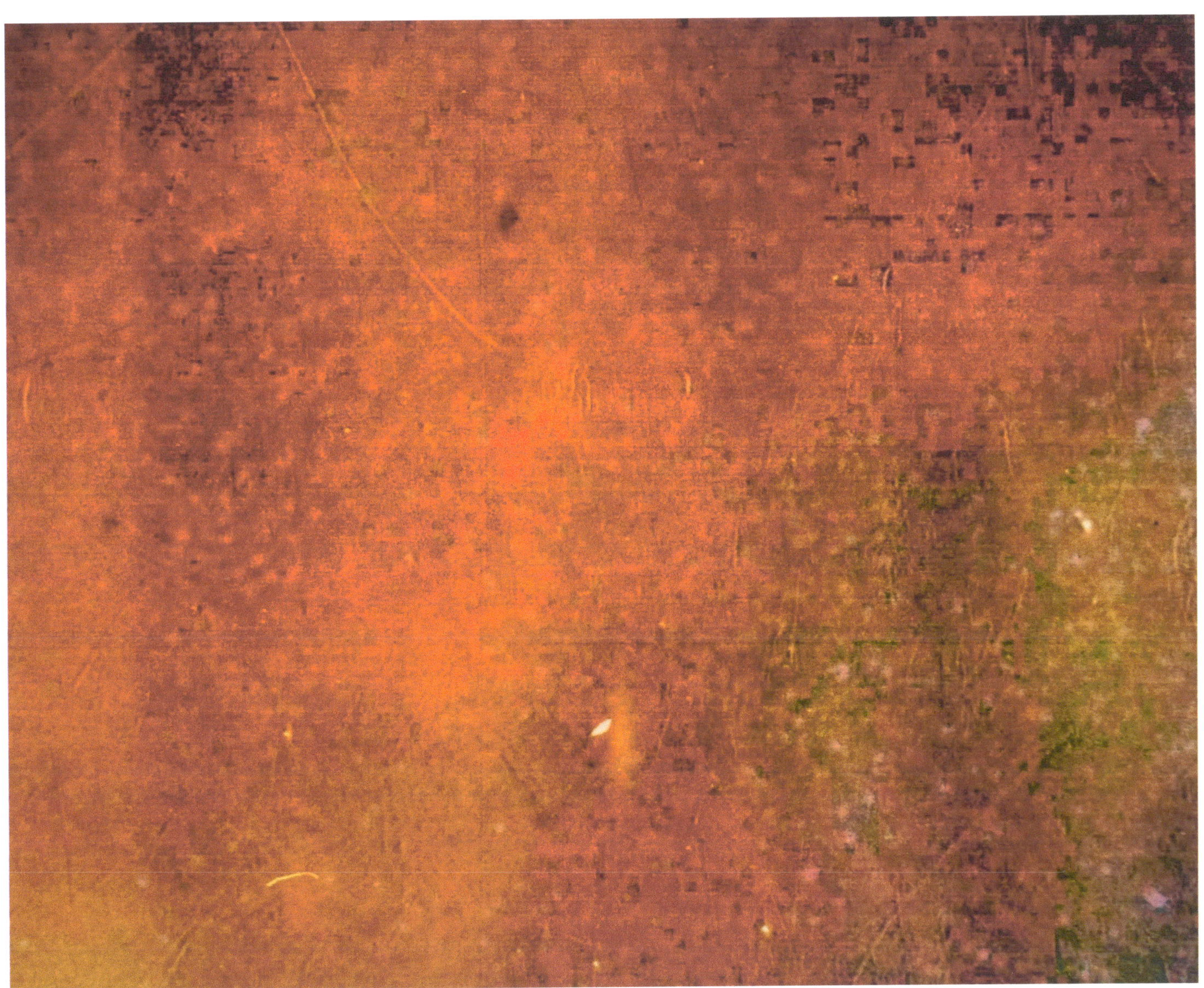

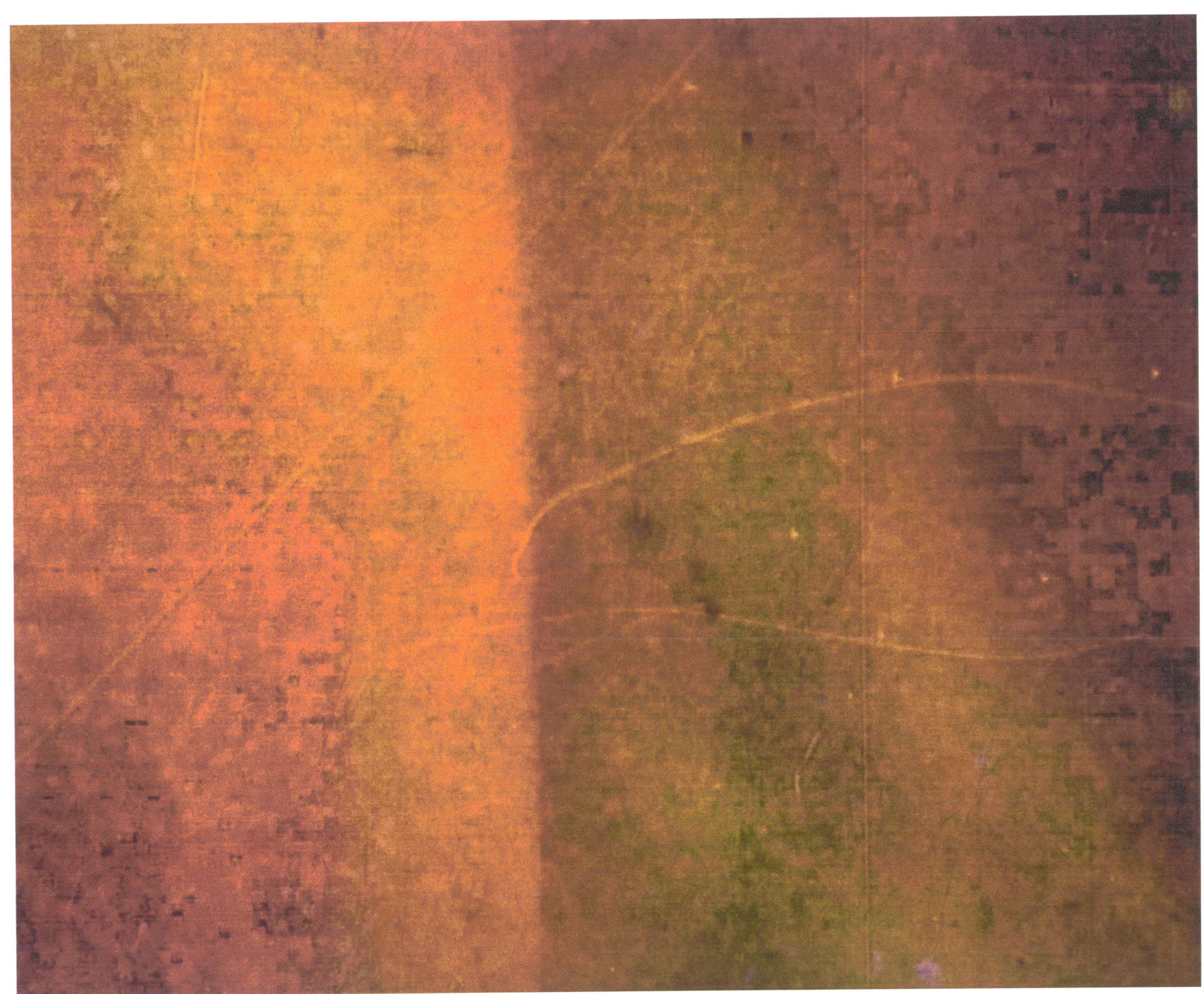

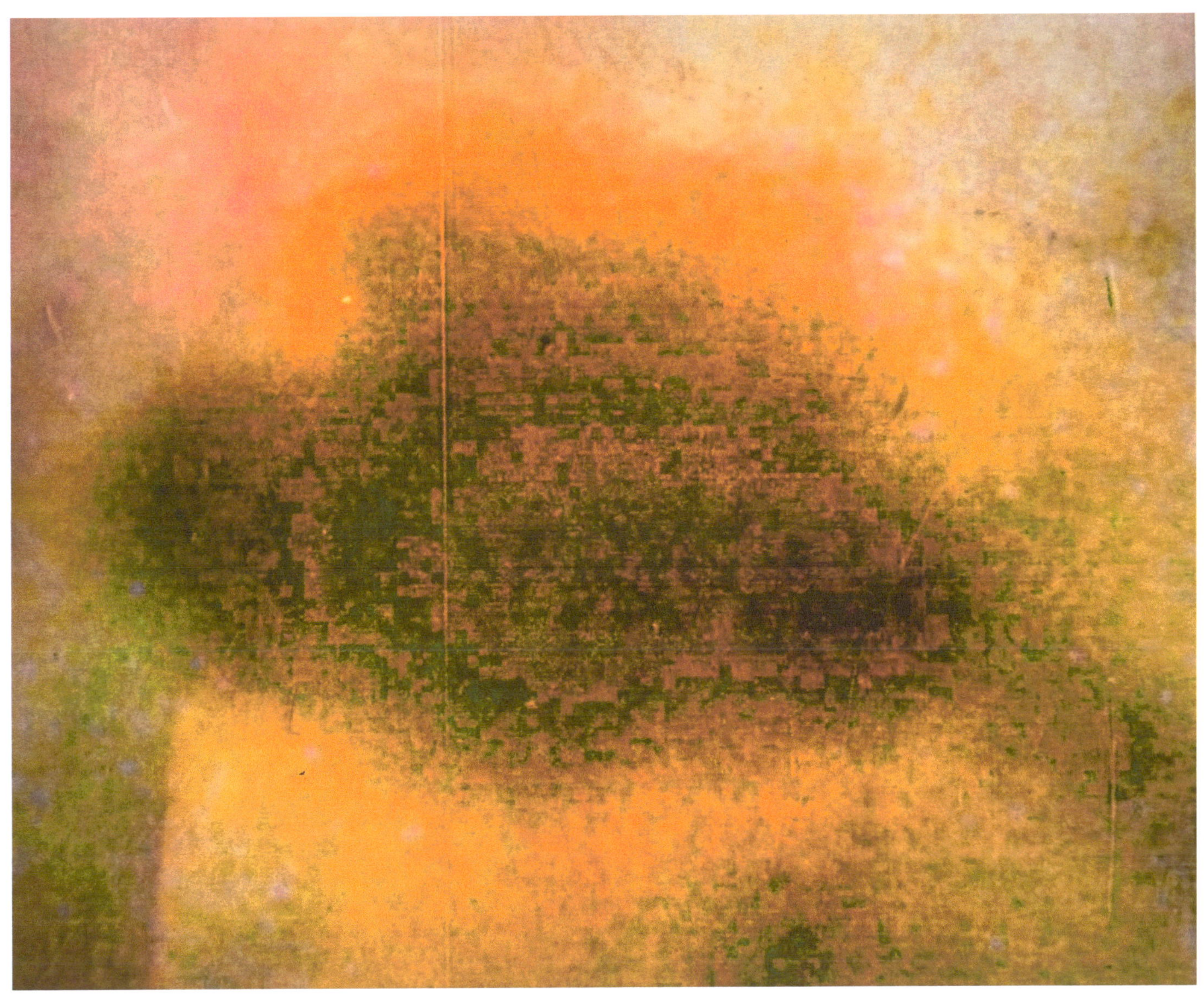

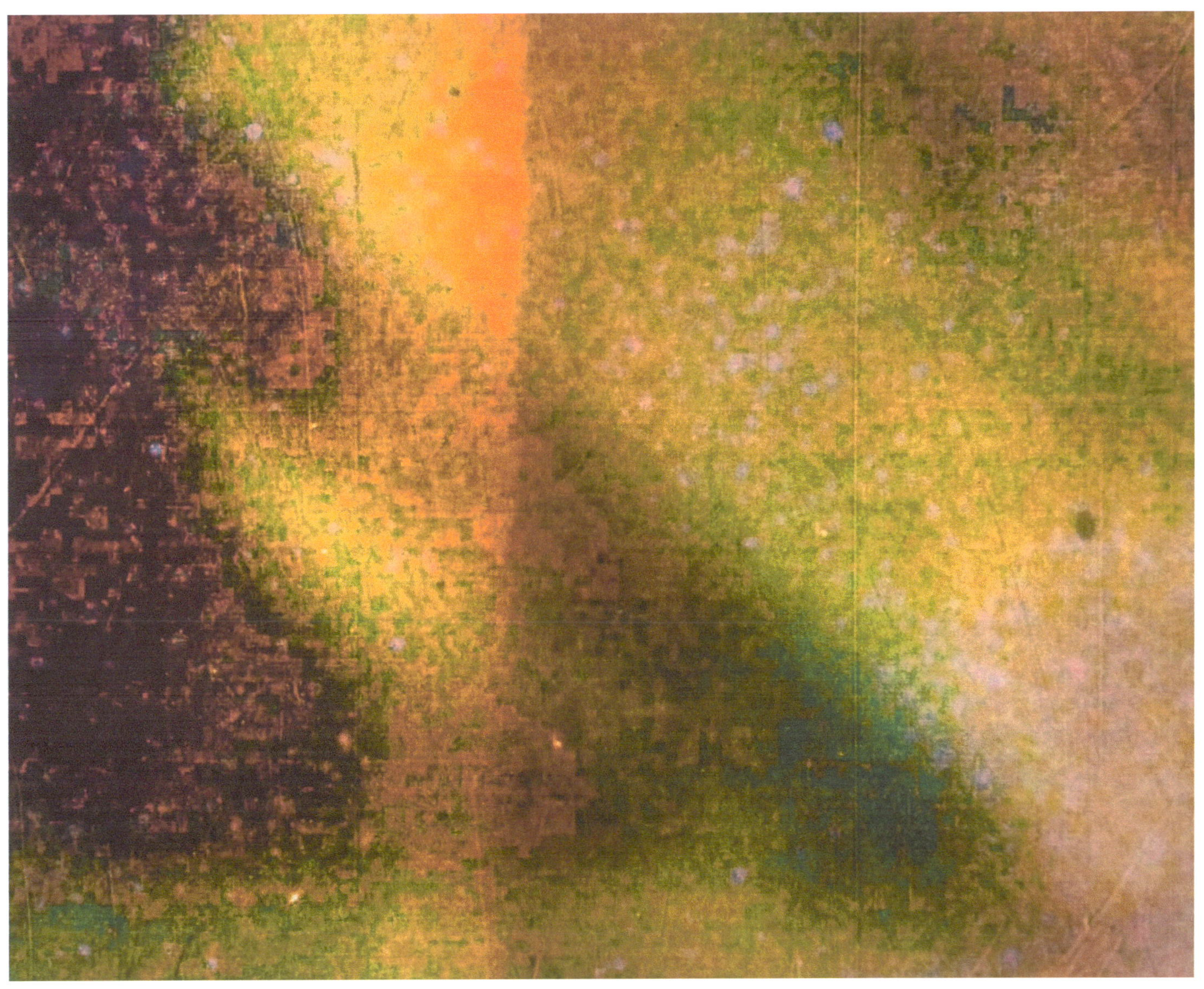

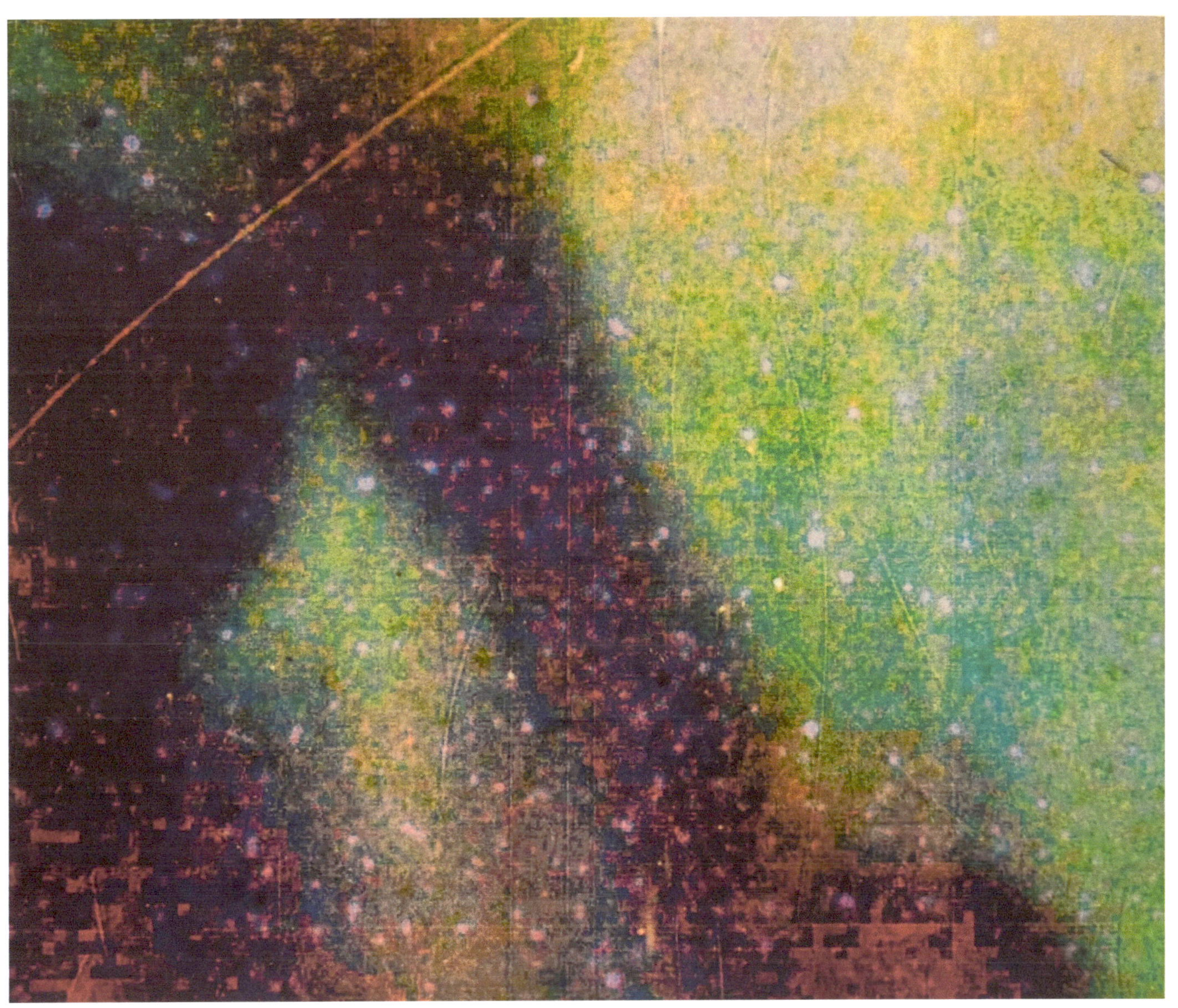

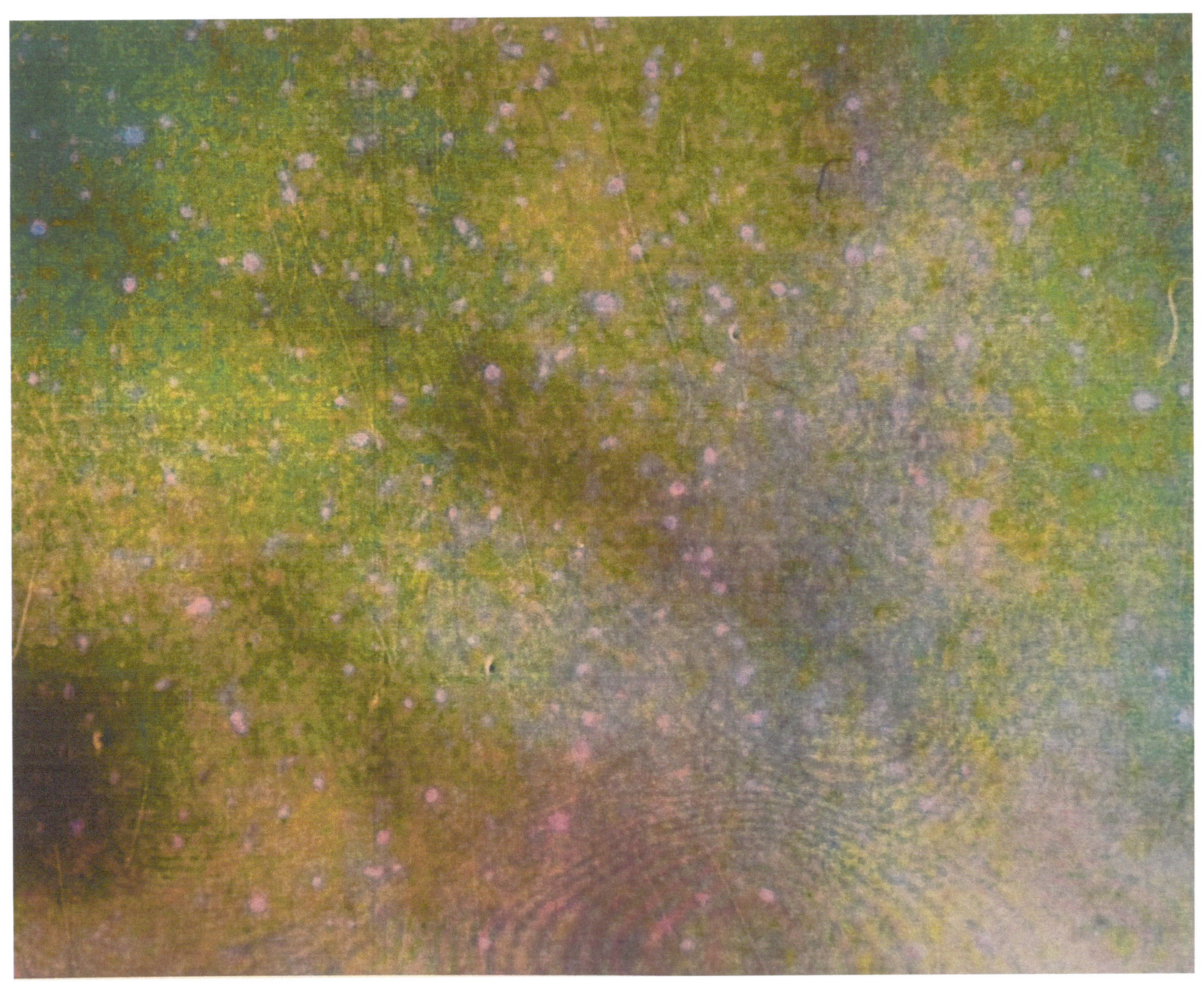

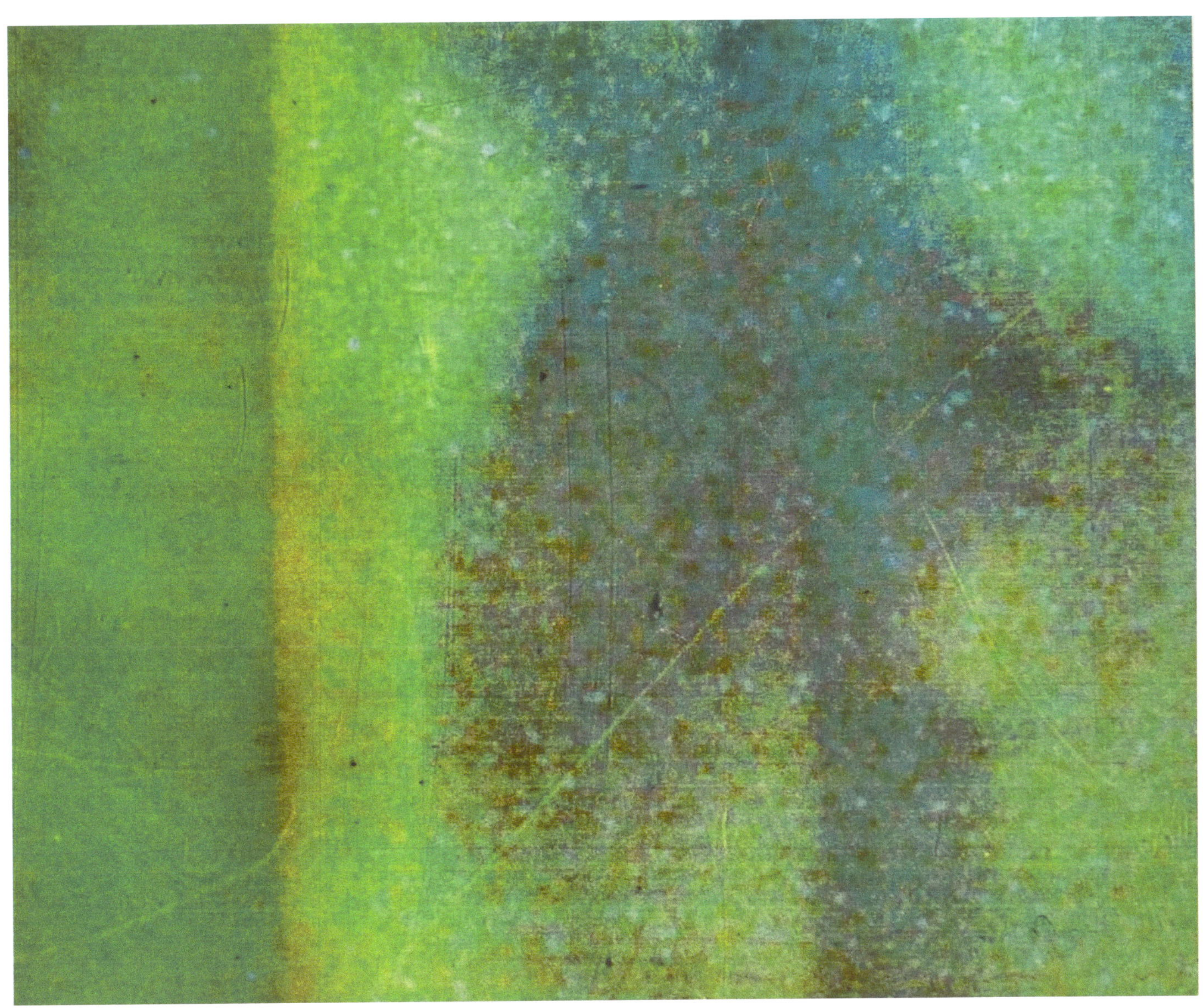

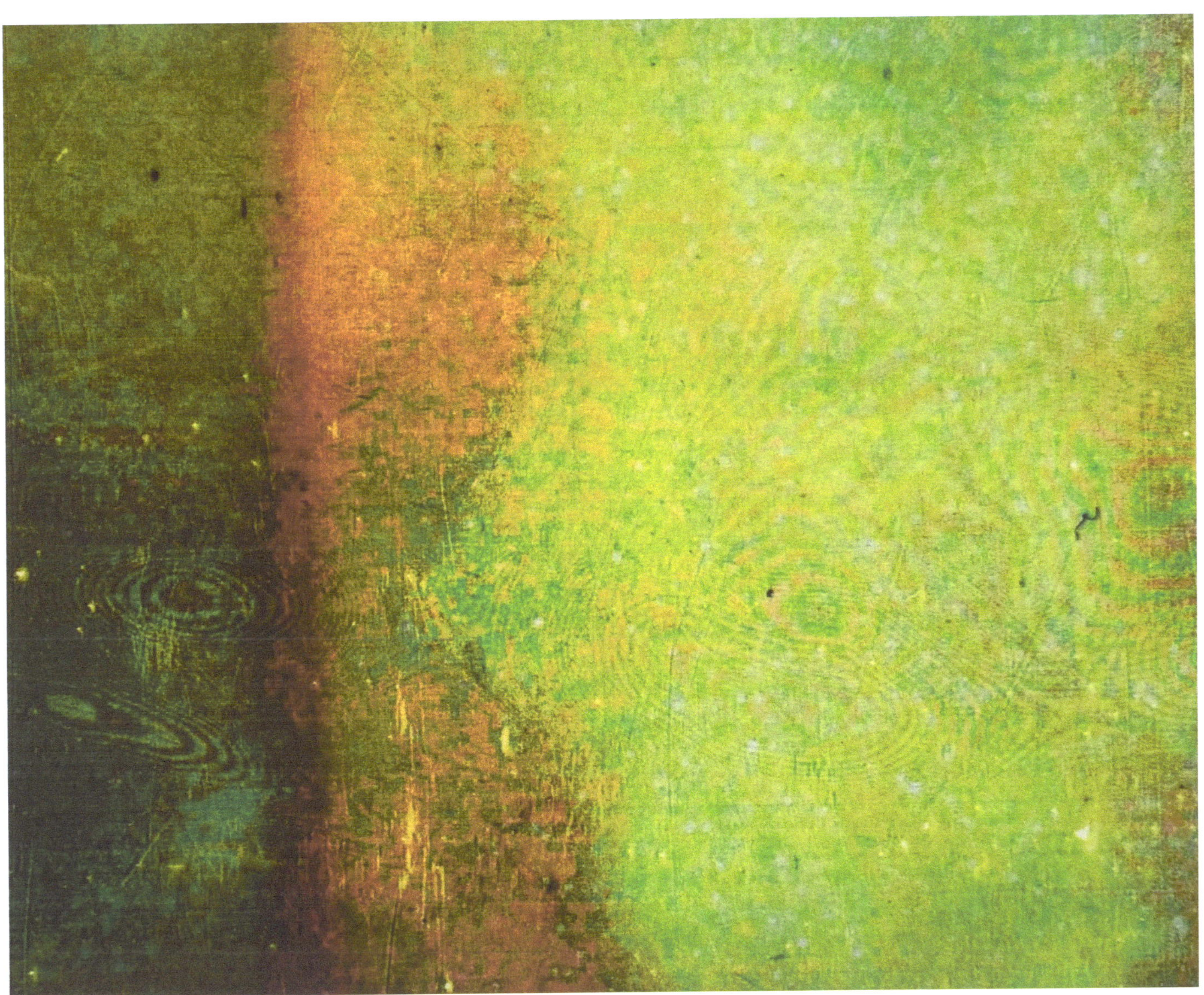

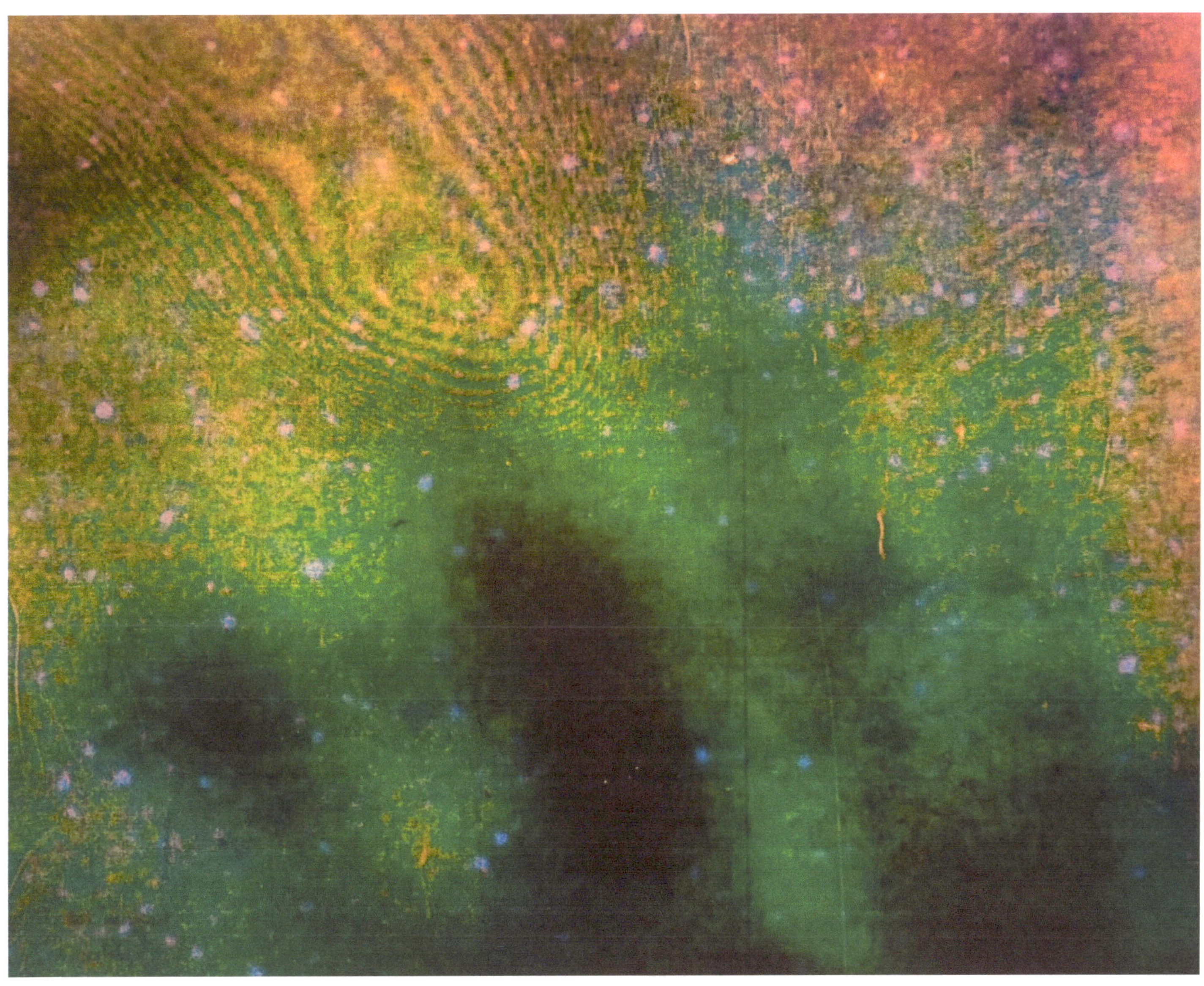

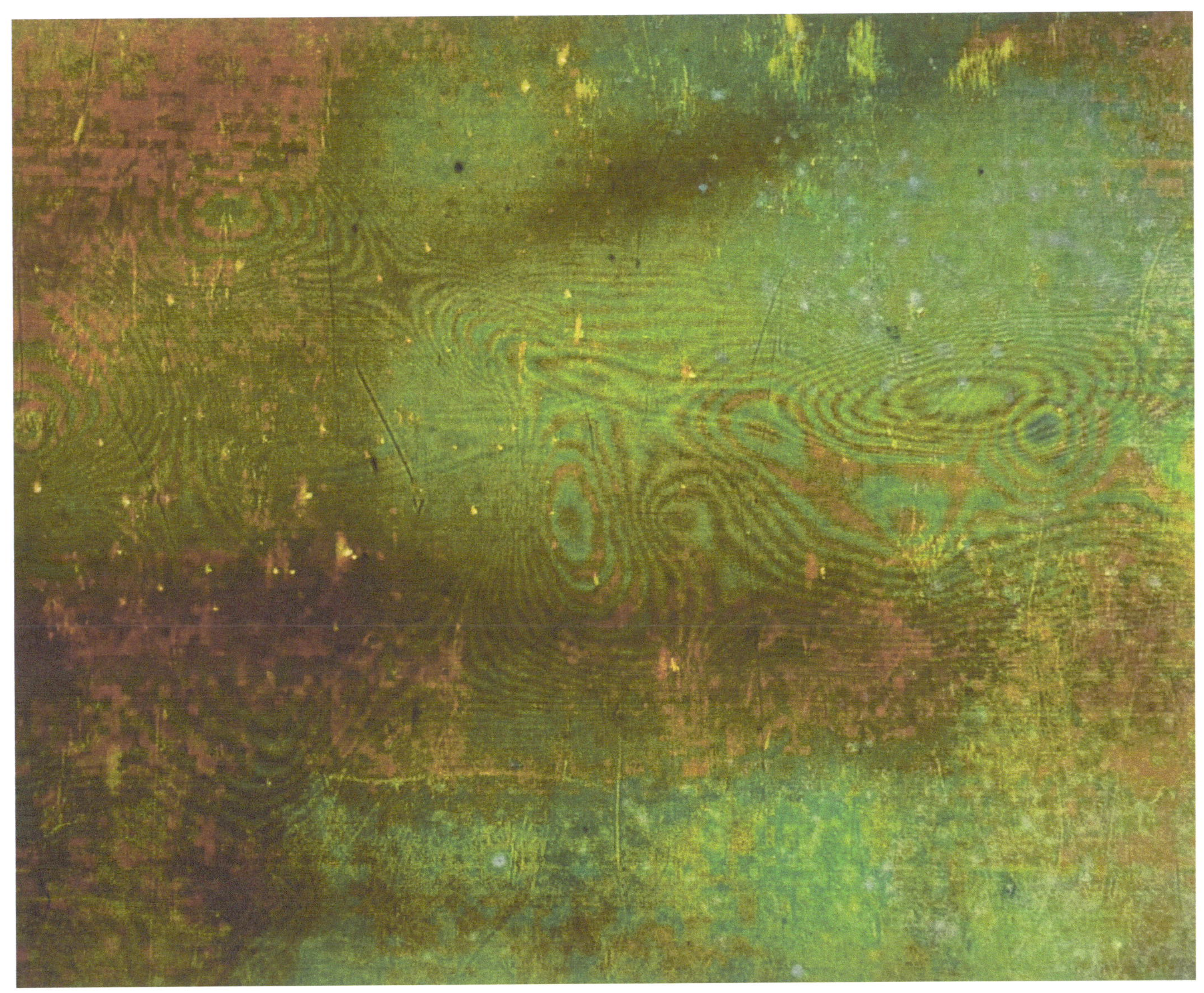

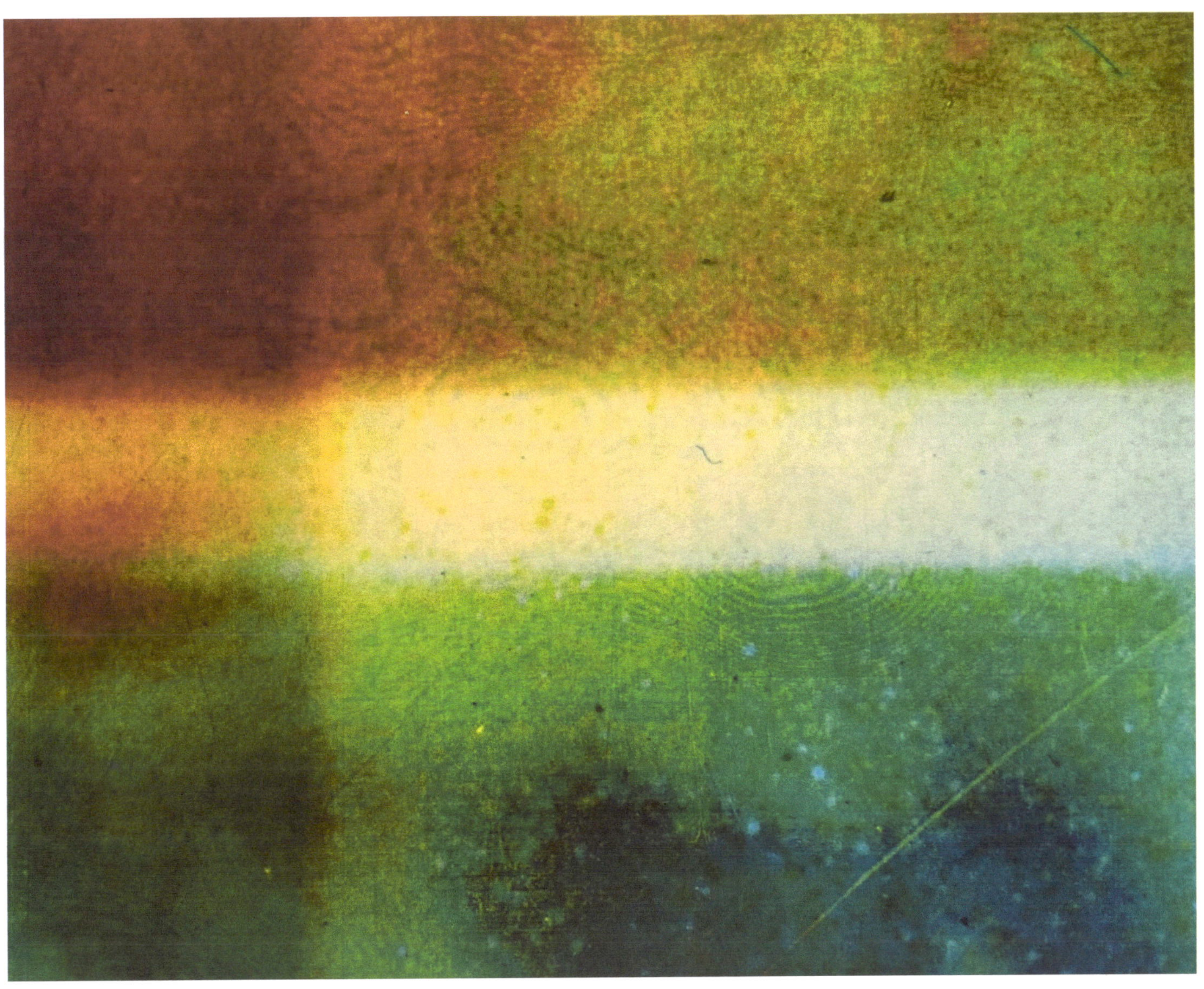

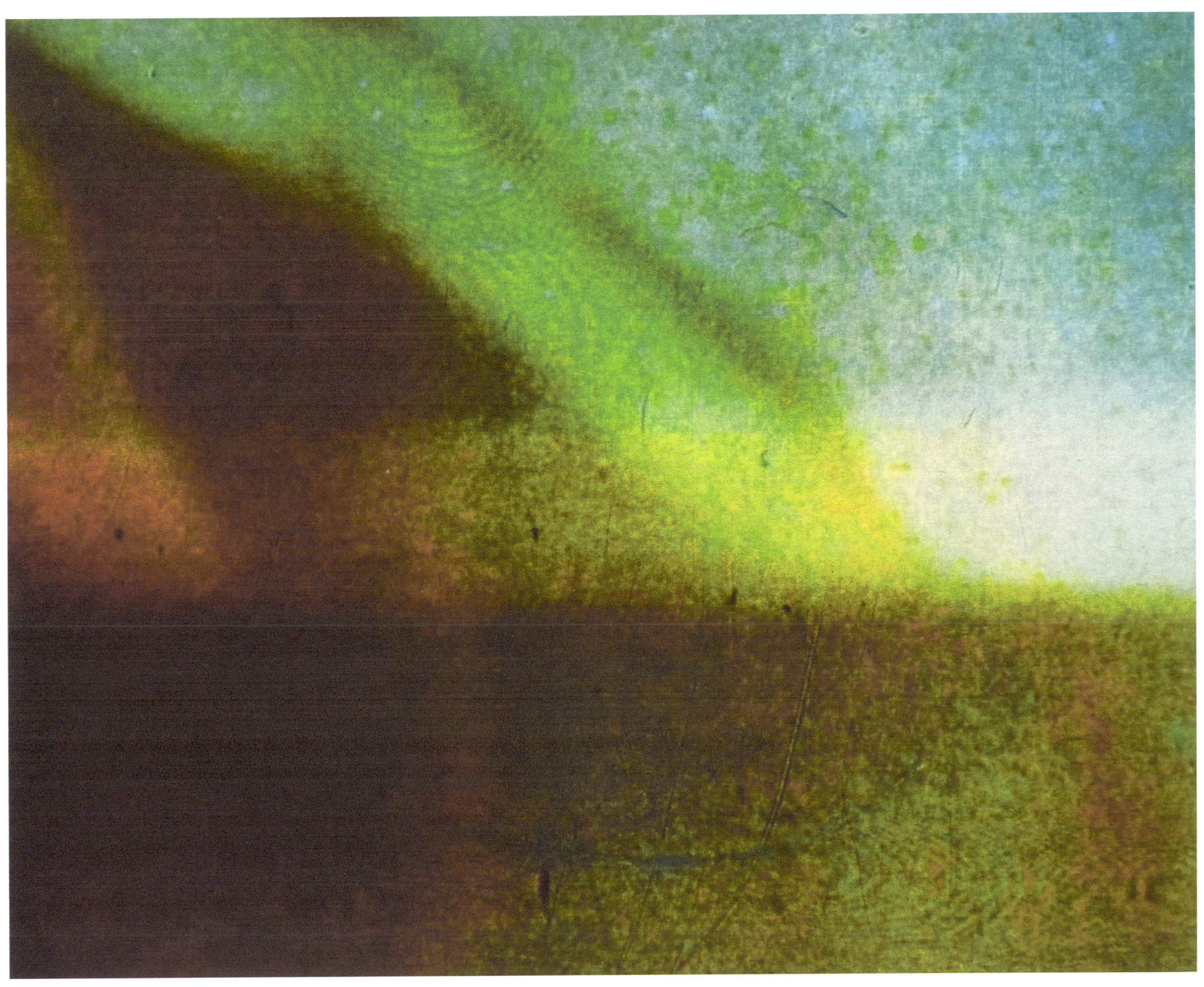

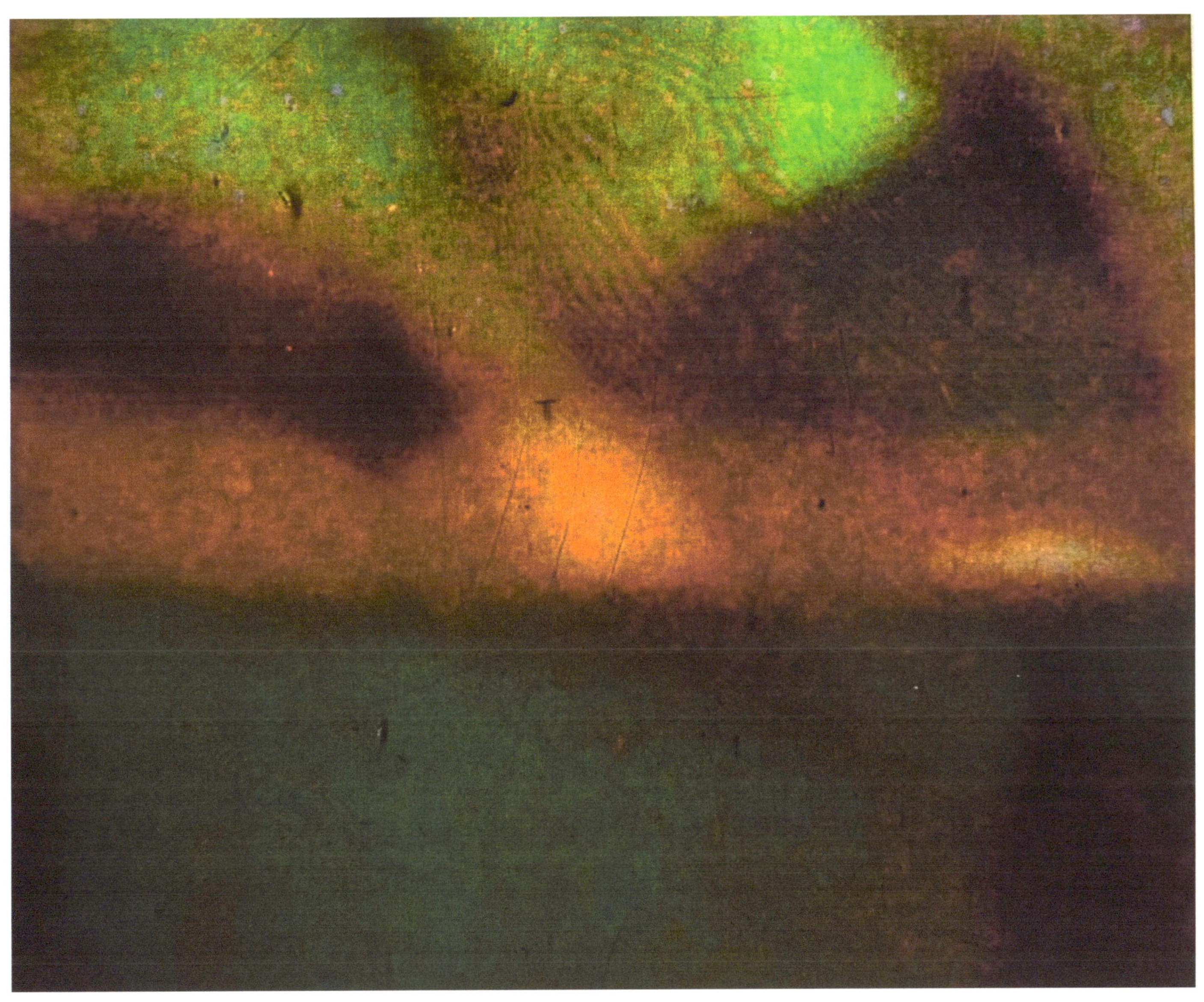

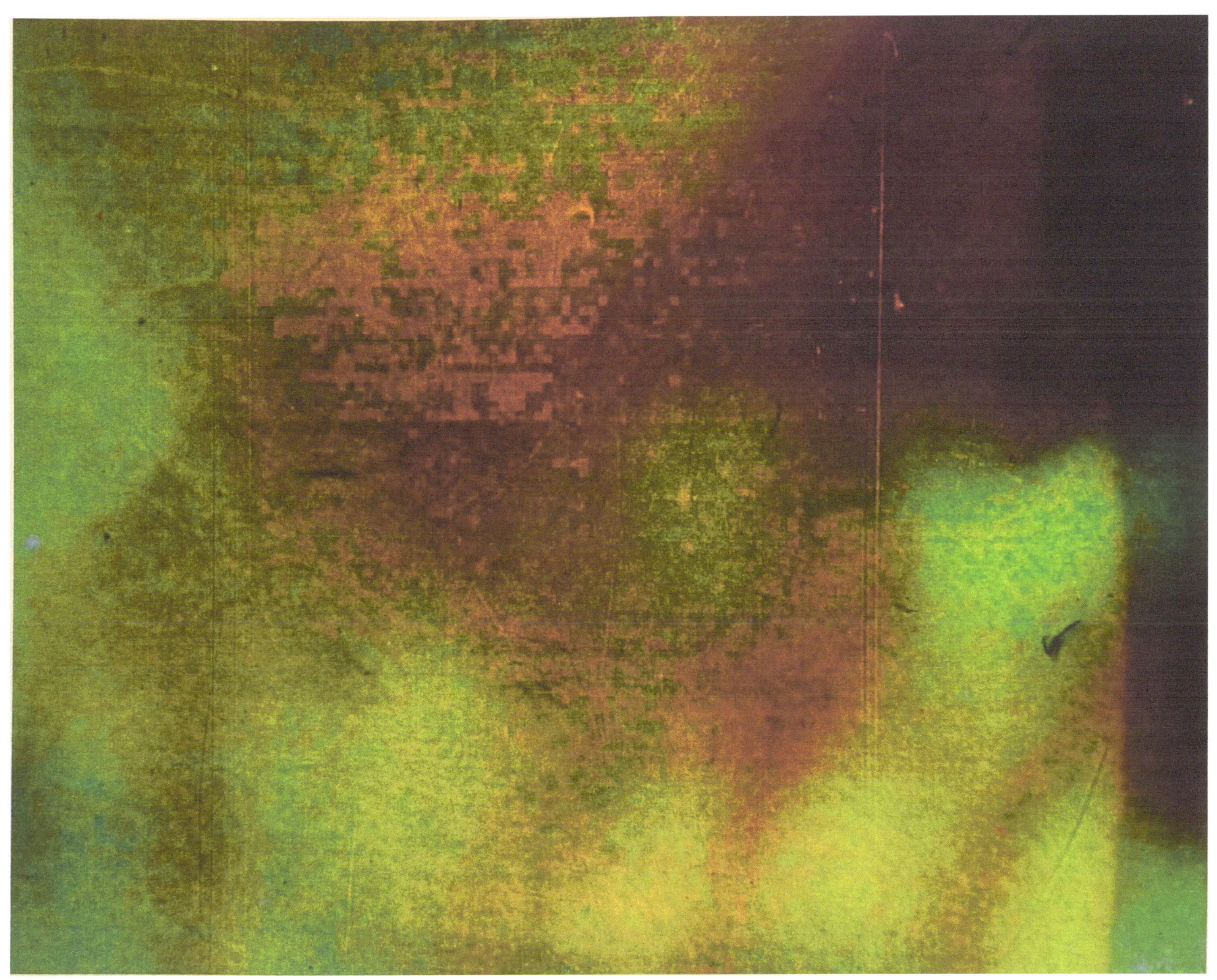

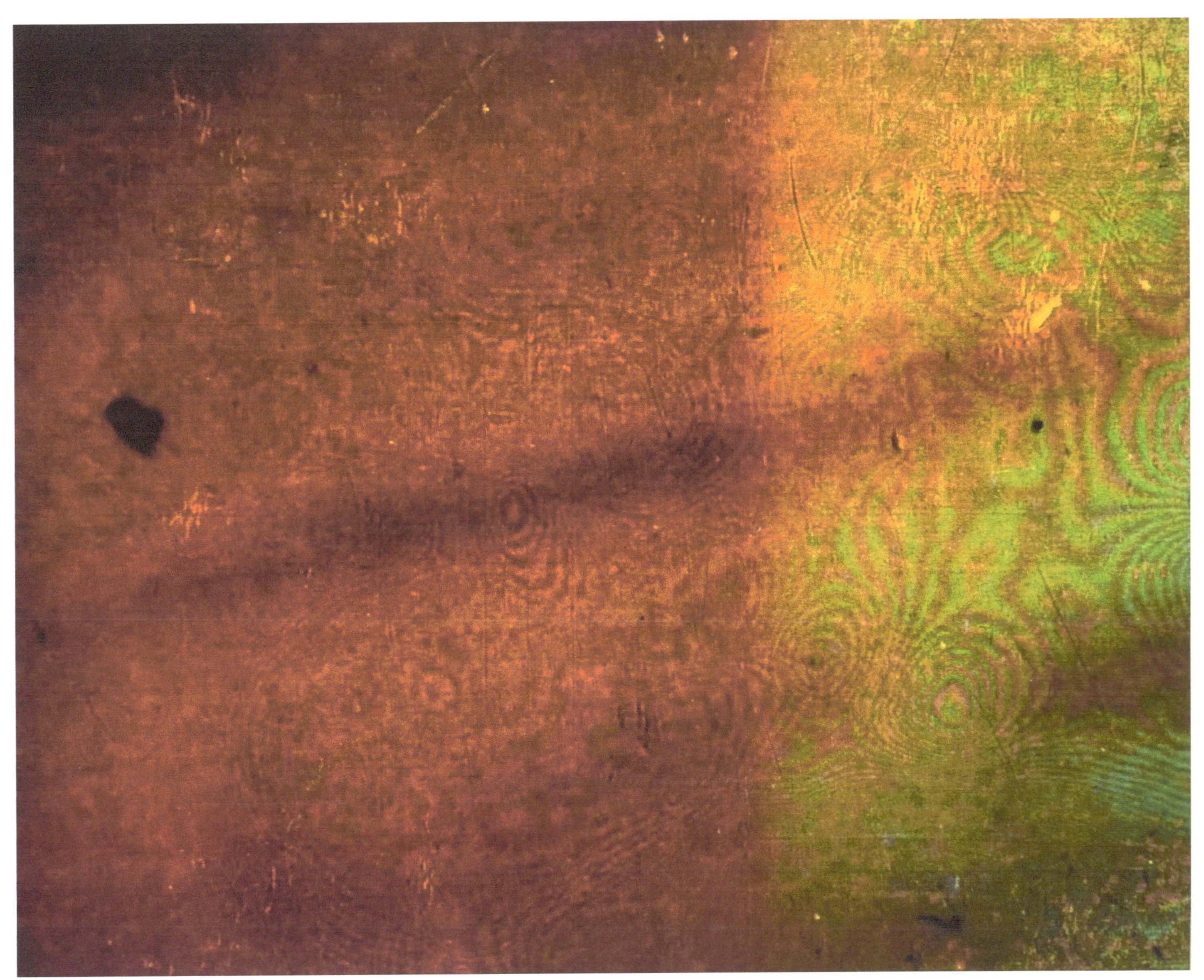

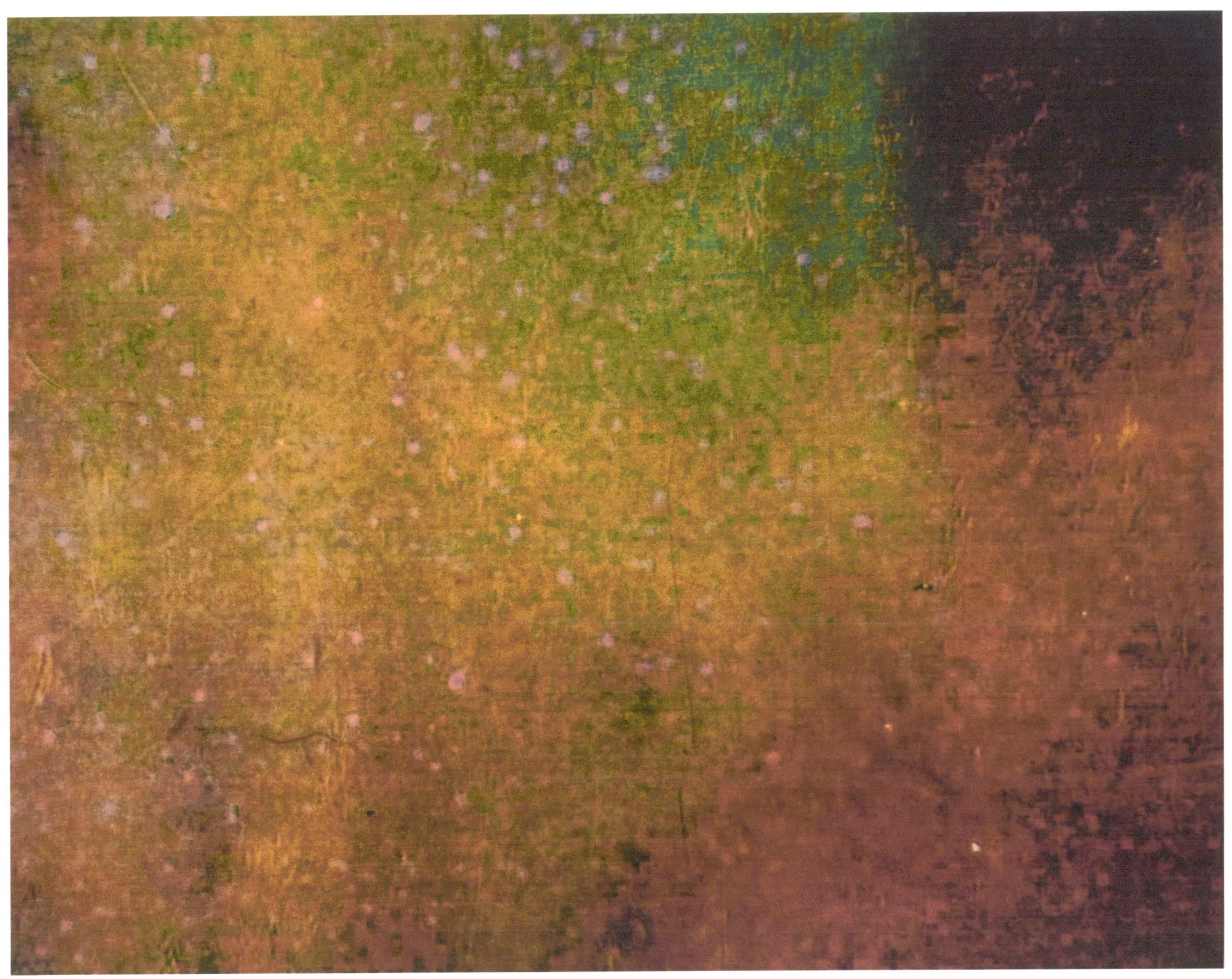

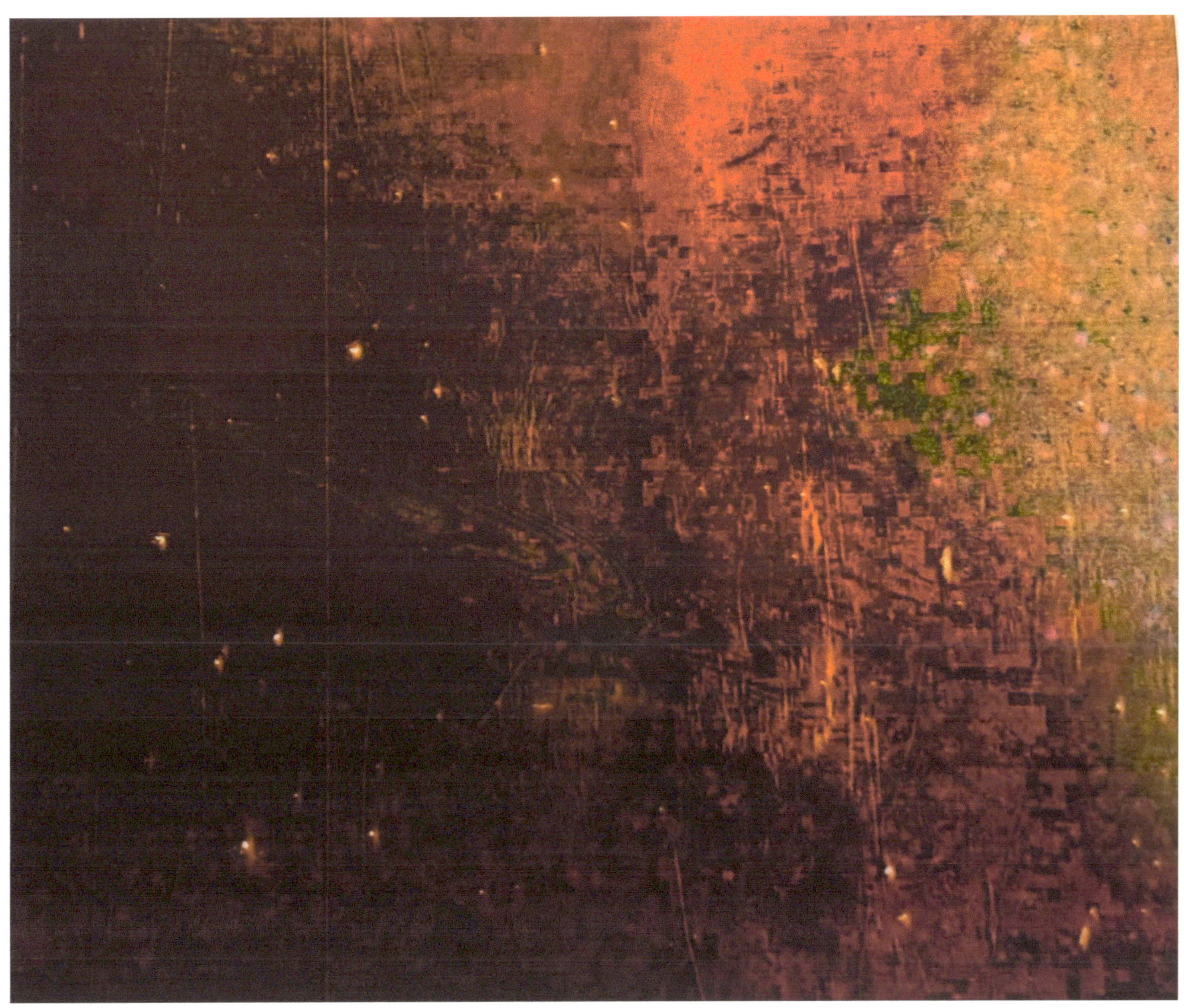

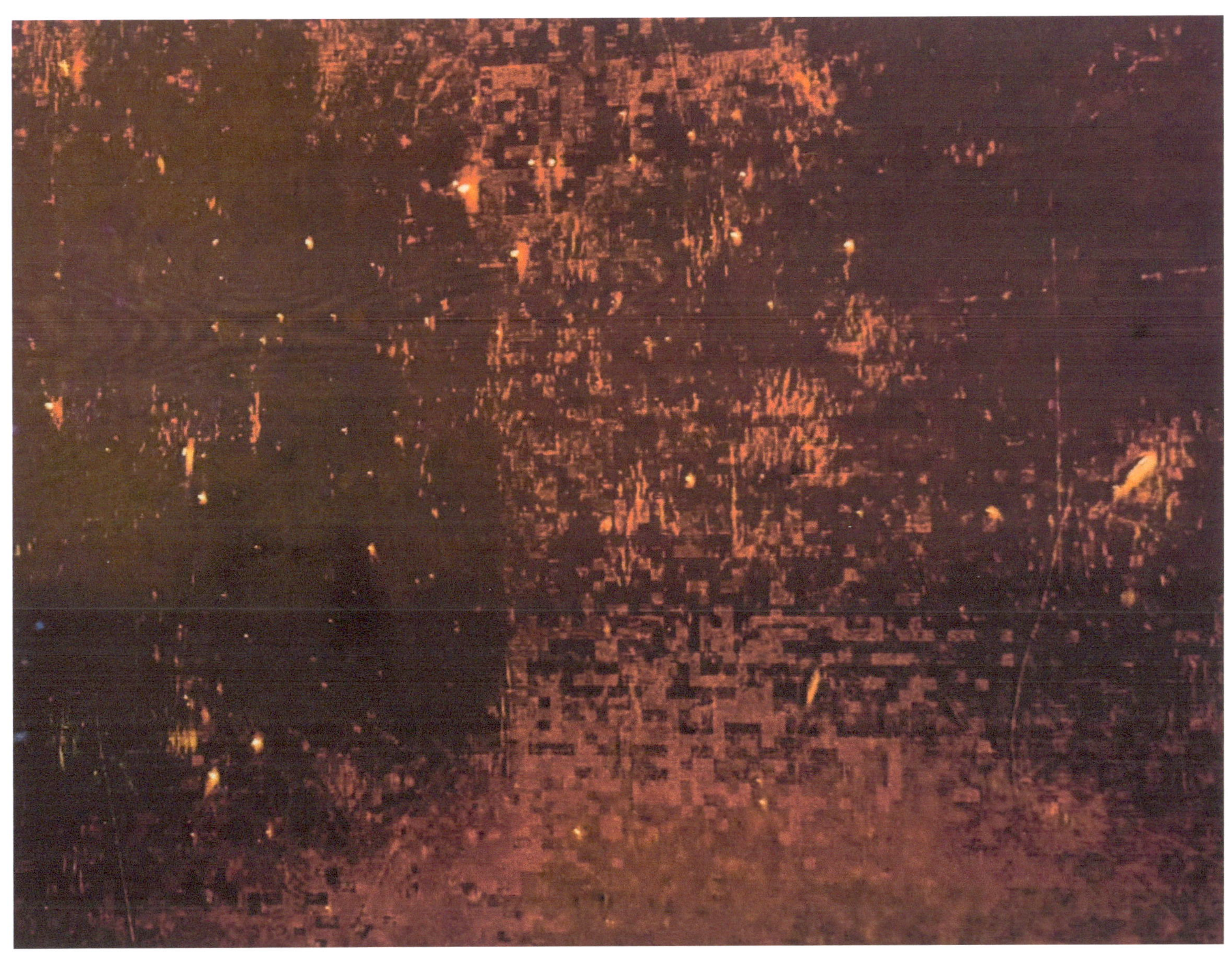

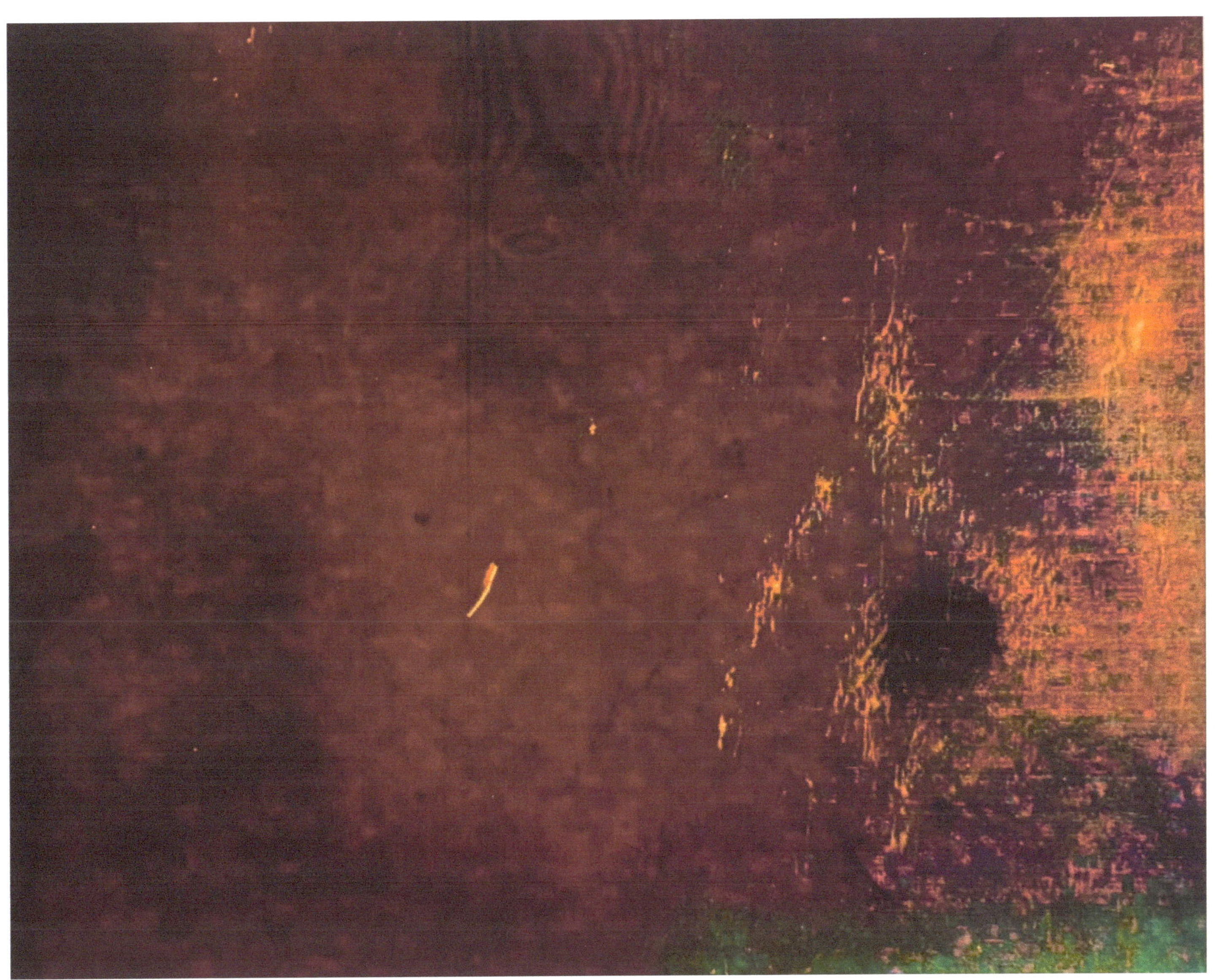

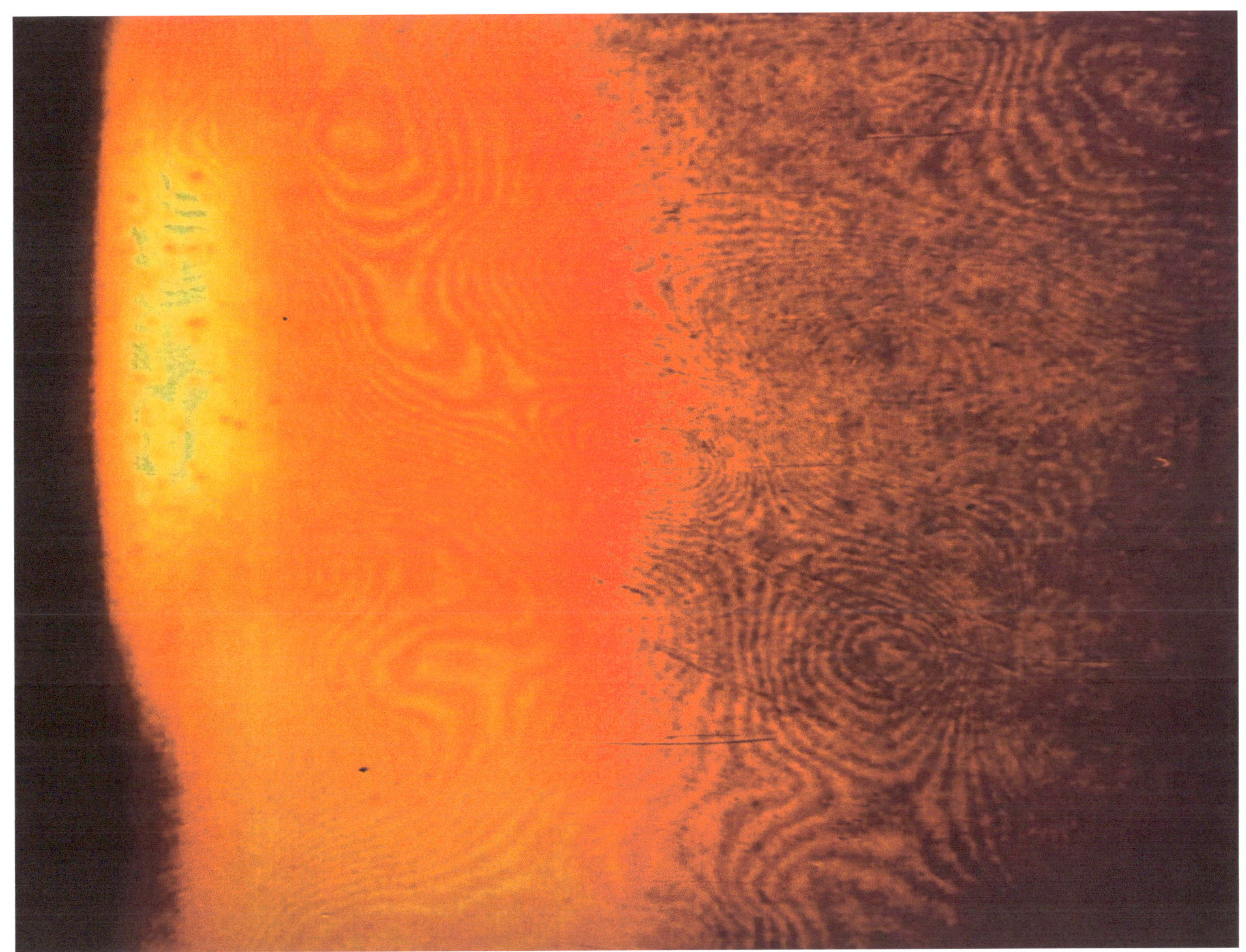

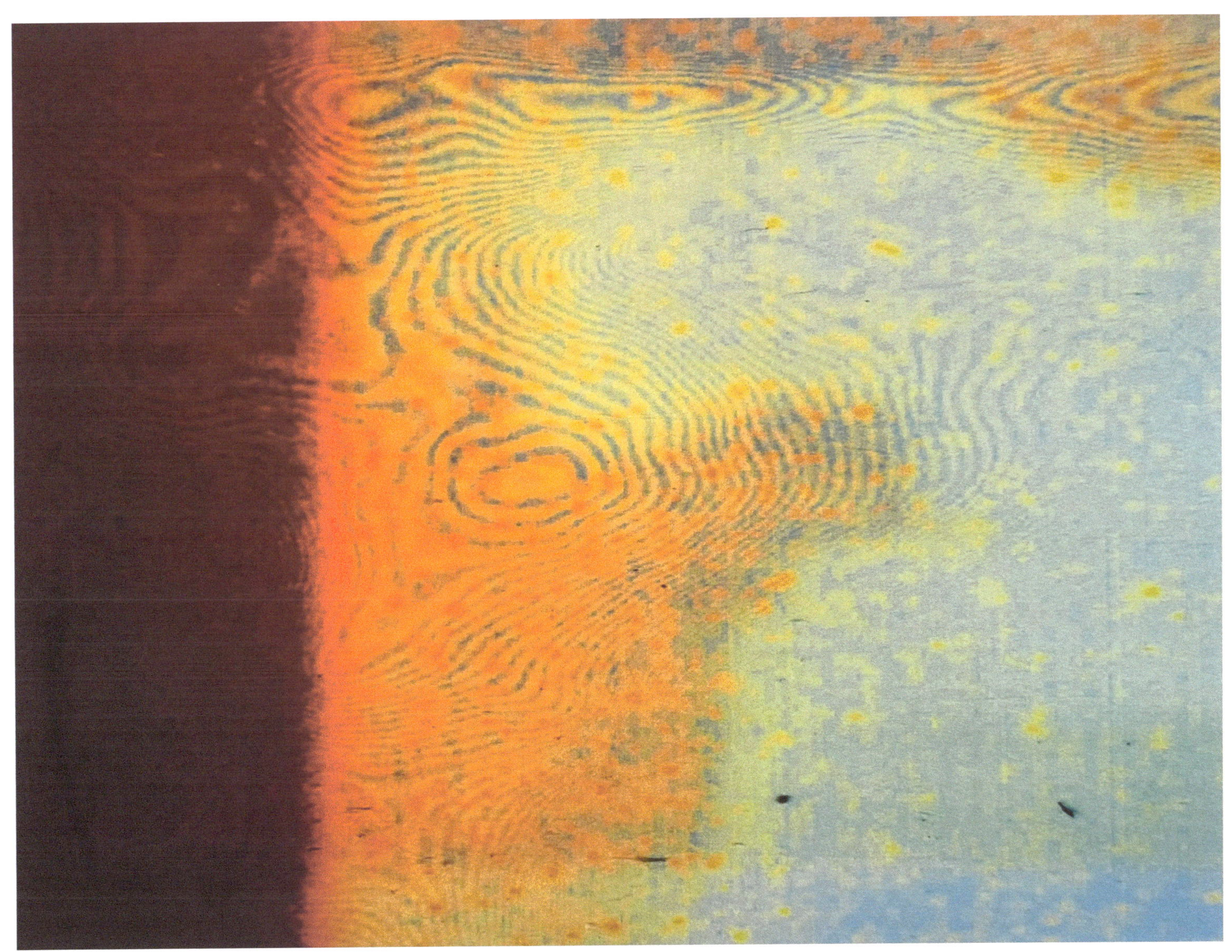

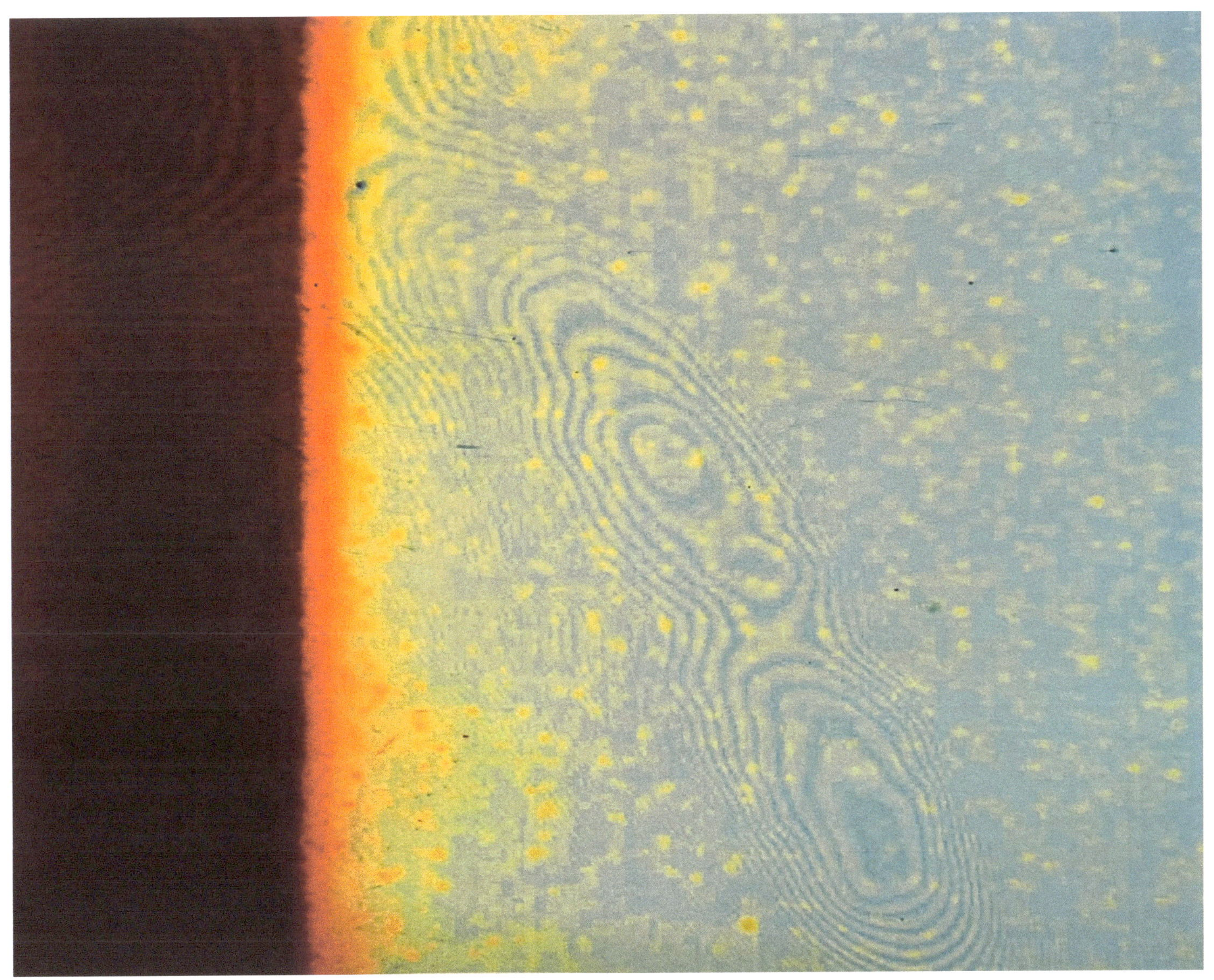

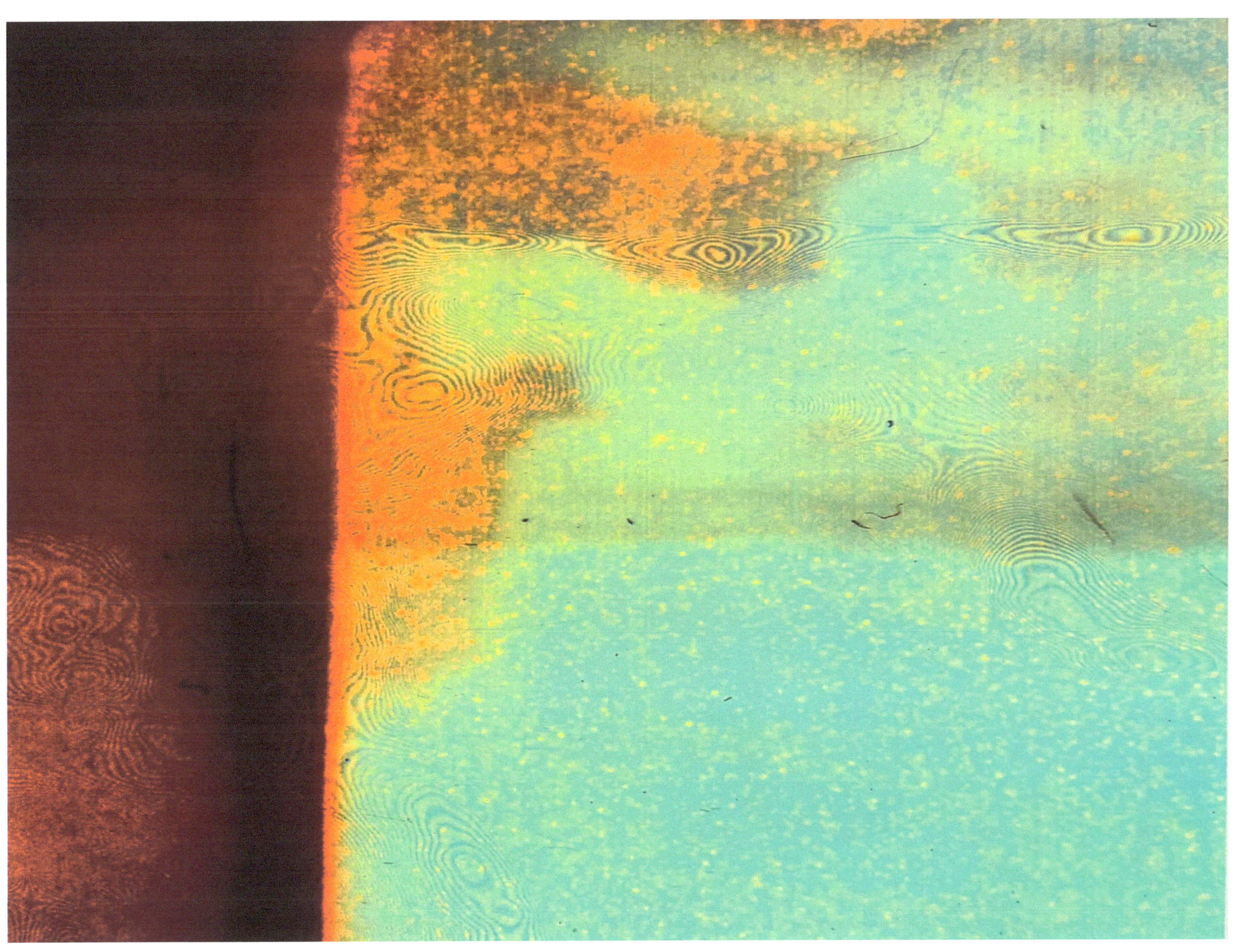

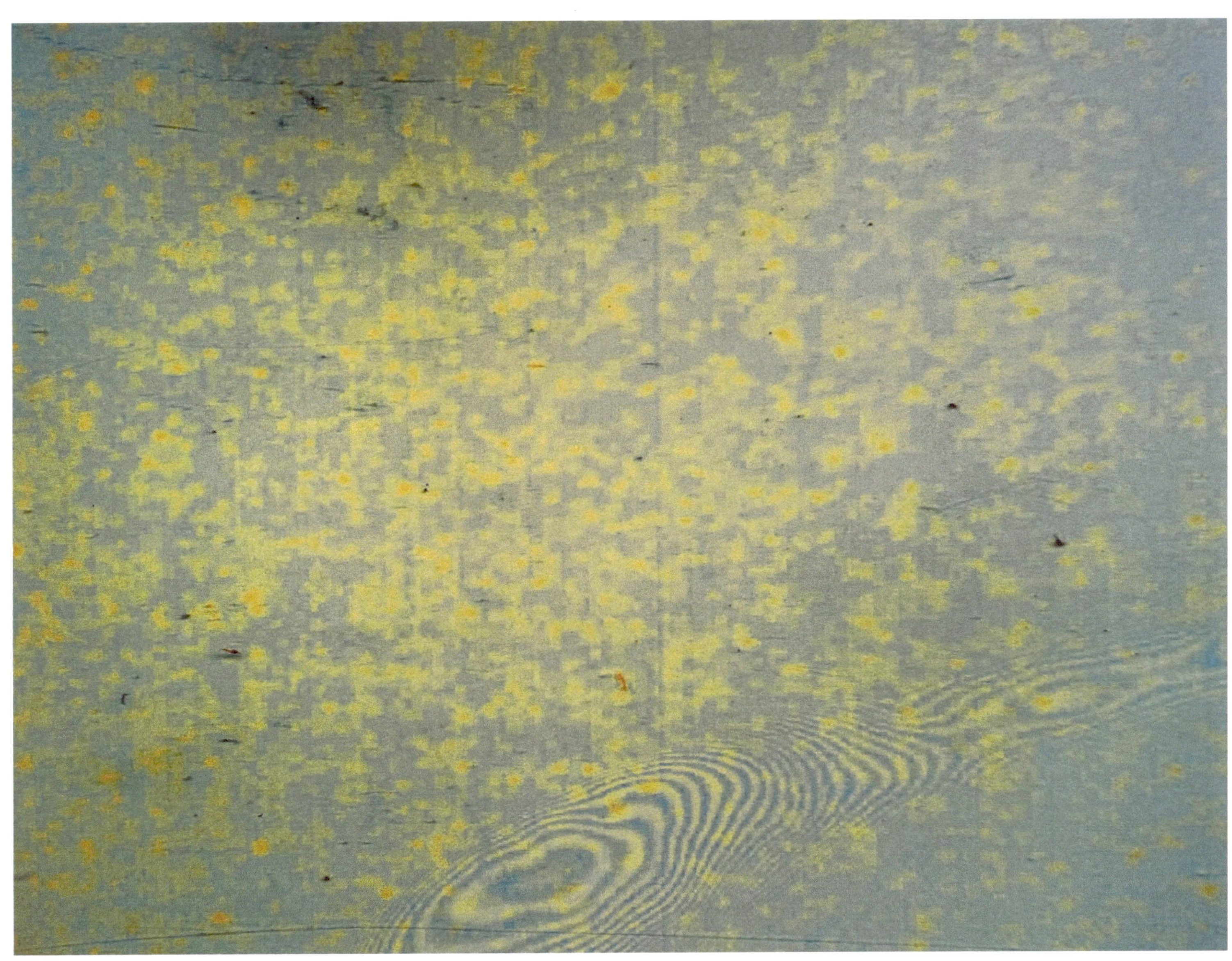

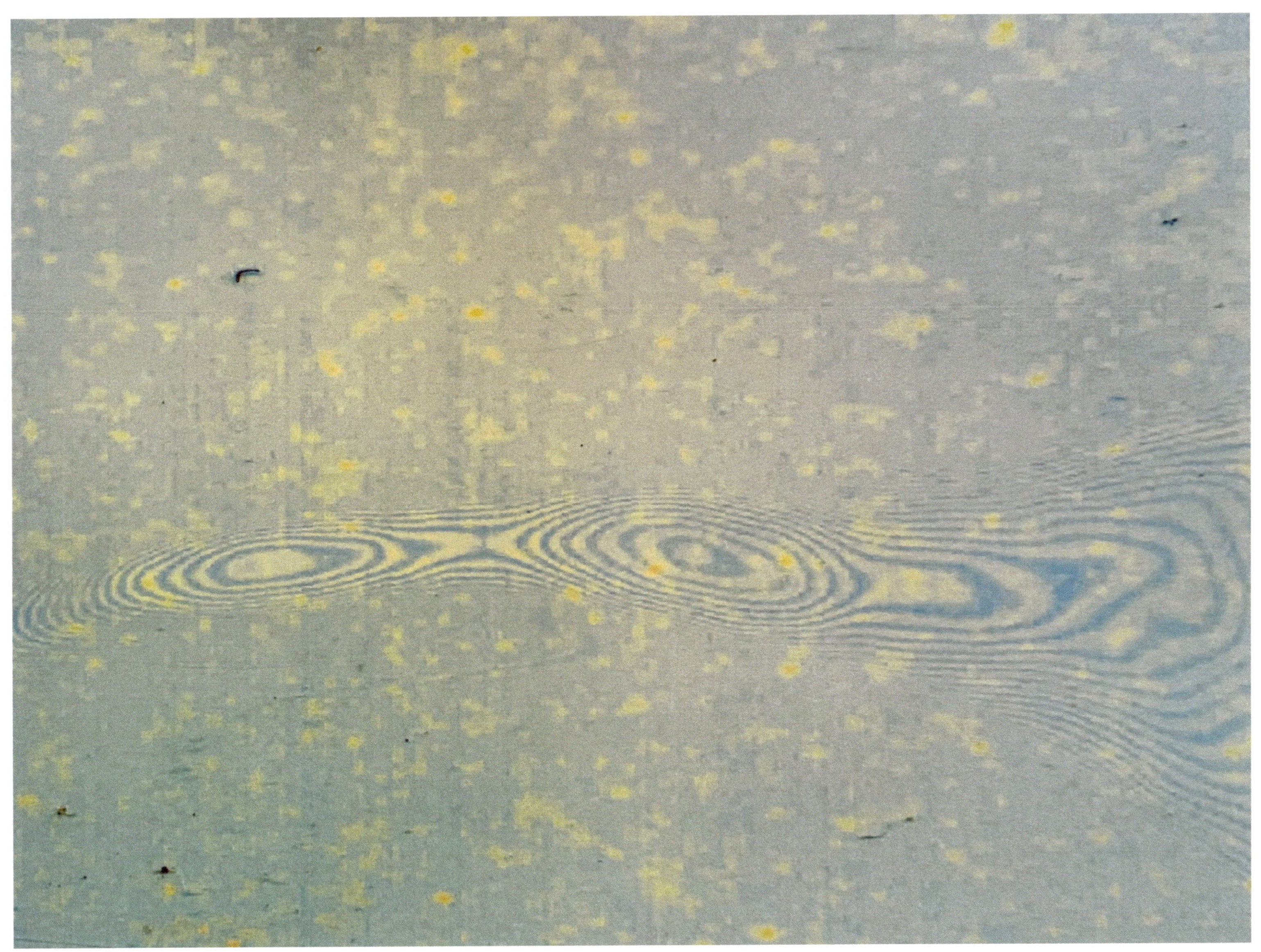

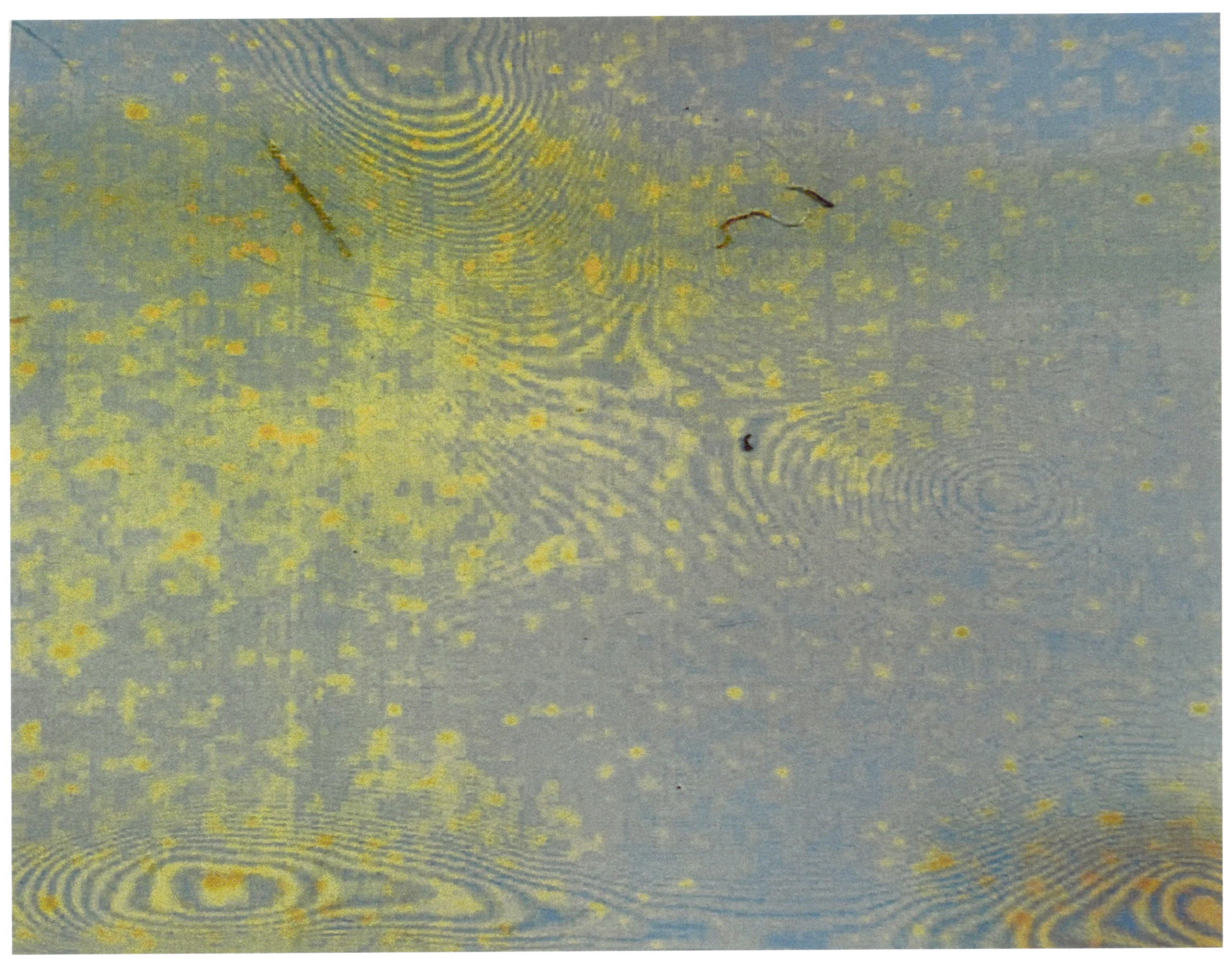

In making this book, I used three land camera photos that came out "wrong" and combined them with digital processes to focus on the chemical and mechanical marks the camera leaves on the film. By taking advantage of these photos that came out "wrong" I was able to focus solely on the color field that these images created. The age of the film caused the colors to be distorted, and allowed the chemical and mechanical processes of the camera to shine through.

What I thought were mistakes, turned out to be the focus of an entire photo book.

These images allow the eye to see whatever they want. In an effort to create images for our brain to process, we end up creating a picture from a series of dots and marks. Like seeing shapes in the clouds, these images allow our mind to create whatever it is our subconscious wants to see.

These images become individualized, special for each viewer based on their experiences in life and simply what their brain can dream up.